Newton's Wildlife Adventures: The Old Mill Pond

Written by
Stephanie Correll

Concept and Illustrations
Simon Knott

Dedication

To My partner Yvonne and My Family,
especially My brother Adam, Without Whom
this book Would Not have been achieved.

THIS BOOK BELONGS to

Newton's Wildlife Adventures: The Old Mill Pond

Today was just like any other day down by the old mill. The leaves were swirling down from the tree tops and the blue sky was breaking through the white puffs of cloud.

Newton, the great crested newt, dived into his favourite place-home! Home was the pond down by the old mill; all of Newton's friends loved the pond as it had so much to offer, so much beauty.

Newton had many friends to keep him company by the poolside, they included 'Pelo' the marsh frog, 'Warton' the natterjack toad and a bunch of cheeky daphnia who would always be lead into trouble by head flea 'Sim'.

The pond where Newton lives is next to an abandoned mill which is part of an active farm. Broken bricks and rusty cogs, from tractors and machinery that time forgot, was all that remained of this once busy mill, but humans still remained on the farm unaware of the creatures that lived in their midst.

A series of streams connecting to the pond had recently become clogged with blanket weed. The pond weed consisted of fine layers of hair like algae, forming a thick blanket over the water's surface, blocking the sunlight and stopping the fresh flow of water from running into the ponds.

The pond water was getting very murky and Newton was not the only one who was less than impressed about this.

The other friends were also uninspired by the mess forming in the water, growing bigger and hairier.

Warton grunted, *"what will we do Newton? What is making our pond water so dirty?"*

Newton thought for a second.

"Maybe we could send you Warton and your friend Pelo, to go have a look at the stream and see what the cause of the problem is."

Newton mentioned to Warton that he had a feeling that it could be Blanket weed that was clogging the water system and that they would have to work as a team if they were going to resolve the issue that was threatening their very existence.

"Why would you think the problem was the pond weed?" asked Warton to Newton.

Newton smirked, "that stuffs been drifting around for days. Poor Argy the water spider hasn't been able to catch any of his tadpoles for a few days now; he keeps trying to fish but, he loses his worms and then the tadpoles hide under the cover of the blankets of weed.

But I never thought it would get so bad as to clog the streams and effect our home, maybe we should have been more wise, we should have intervened much sooner."

Warton said to Newton with raised eyebrows, *"Oh sure thing Newton, we wouldn't mind looking, I'll just go fetch Pelo, I think he is down by the mill right now."*
So Warton the toad headed down to meet Pelo the frog, so they could do some investigating of their own.

Pelo was already near the mill and the friends made the journey down to the old mill pond and farm together, to see what was wrong with the streams that seemed to be affecting the pond in which they lived.

When they arrived at the scene, they discovered the Daphnia and started making conversation with them to see if they could shed any light on the situation.

The Daphnia explained to the two friends that they were trying to create a vegetable patch to grow some horse tails, a water plant for their community, when they had an accident with the fertiliser,

"We wanted to make the biggest and tastiest Horse Tails we could."

Pelo interrupted the conversation to say, *"but, why did you not let anyone know of this mishap? It could have been a nasty risk to the waterways."*

The Daphnia said, *"Well, we had good intentions; we only wanted to do well, but we can be very clumsy at times and a bit cheeky, I guess we didn't think this through."*

Pelo and Warton looked at one another realising that Newton had said he spotted Blanket Weed and now they knew how it grew so vigorously; it started to grow out of control due to the fertiliser getting into the streams.

They turned to the Daphnia and said, "You lot will need to work together and help us clear the weed and algae entirely, so we can return to a natural co-existence."

The Daphnia said, *"Oh, but we don't want to tidy up; playing with the pond weed is just too much fun, throwing it about, watching it splash and seeing the ripples cascade in the stream."*

Warton said, *"We could use the buckets from the old abandoned mill. I think I saw some when I went past there the other week, I could see what else is down there."* The gang cheered, *"Sure Warton, let's do this!"*

Warton headed down to the Old Mill where he bumped into Neom the water shrew, a very close friend of his, who was always out and about. Neom was a nosey shrew who liked to gossip, but he was very harmless.

Warton smiled at Neom and they both exchanged hellos, then with an eager smile Neom asked Warton how he was.

"Oh I am fine Neom, just about to carry out some cleaning duties. The water in the streams has got clogged up quite badly with Blanket weed and it has basically taken over our home."

Neom looked shocked and replied hastily, *"I must lend a hand to you and your friends Warton, I didn't realise our home had got in such a bad state, I was away visiting family."*

The two set off as fast as they could. Extra hands were always welcome when a big project was on the cards.

The friends arrived at the Old Mill which had been left empty for many years, the wood was worn, the bricks where smeared with history and overgrown with grass as high as the sky. The Old Mill was thriving with life.

They made it to the buildings which towered over them, they felt scared of their new surroundings – a place that had always been close to home, but somewhere they never thought to venture to until now.

They hurried around the great structure, dusting every corner in search of tools to help their friends with the clean-up; always remembering in the back of their minds that time was of the essence.

Warton shouted over to Pelo, *"I have found some buckets sat next to some rusty rakes, but this actually might be better as we need something to collect the weeds with."*

Pelo told Warton, "Well done for finding the equipment, maybe we should head back, meet the Daphnia and go down to the pond to sort this mess out."

On returning to the streams to meet the Daphnia, Pelo, Neom and Warton met head flea Sim. They were so annoyed with all their efforts that had been used to correct the foolery of the Daphnia that they stood slumped as if not impressed by his presence.

Sim could see that Pelo and Warton were less than happy and Neom just looked a bit blank; the day had taken quite a lot out of the three friends.

Sim turned to them with a heartfelt sorrow and said, *"I didn't mean for you to get caught up in this mayhem. You know us Daphnia, we love to play in the pond weed, and it's what makes us who we are. I do understand the concerns you had with the fertiliser, I should have taken quicker action being the leader and all."*

Newton appeared out of nowhere, parting the grass with both hands, when he noticed his friends with the Daphnia and Sim by the Old Mill.

"Pelo, Warton, what took you so long? I was waiting for you to come and collect me to let me know the current situation."

They turned to Newton and did the only thing they really could, they apologised saying, *"the day was a bit more of a challenge than expected, but at least we are altogether now and the work can begin."*

The gang got their buckets and rakes at the ready and cleared away the algae and Blanket weed till every bucket was almost overflowing. The sun started to slowly set and the gang turned to the Daphnia and said, *"Now it's time to eat your food instead of playing with it and causing mischief."*

The waterways were now free to flow again and the family of alder trees stood tall; Senior Ogham, Ogham Junior and Little Eb looked proud of the efforts of their friends and could see the glory that teamwork can bring when we choose to get along for the sake of our world. Newton and his friends could finally relax on their favourite tree branch, having fun until the sun went down.

Argy was happy now that he could finally see through the water and try his hand at fishing again, dangling worms from his makeshift rod, but would he actually catch a tadpole? Well maybe we will find out next time.

Newton's Wildlife Fact File

Common Earthworm
Lumbricus terrestris

This animal is a large invertebrate, reddish in colour and native to Britain and Europe. The Earthworm was introduced to other countries by humans. The common earthworm is also known as a night crawler and is an herbivore.

Marsh Frog/Tadpoles
Pelophylax ridibundus

A native European frog that is aquatic and is always within jumping distance of water. It is also known as the laughing frog due to the calling sound it makes and can reach 17cm in length.

Water spider
Argyroneta aquatica

The water spider is the only species of spider to live solely in water. There lifespan is about two years, they love to live in ponds and eat an array of insects. It is not on the endangered list.

Natter jack Toad
Epidalea calamita

This endangered toad is known to be one of Europe's most noisy amphibians. They are very rare in Britain and these toads are very poor swimmers and will drown if they cannot get ashore.

Great Crested Newt
Triturus cristatus

Britain's largest newt species, they are endangered but now protected due to the destruction of their habitat. They also go by the names of Northern Crested Newt and Warty Newt. The adults breed in the spring in ponds and then emerge onto land during summer to rest.

Great Pond Snail

Lymnaea stagnalis

Widespread throughout Britain and Europe and is found in slow moving or stagnant water. They will eat algae and even rotting organic matter; they take in grains of sand, which stay in their gizzards, to help breakdown plant matter that it may otherwise not be able to digest. They are not endangered.

Water flea
Daphnia

Commonly known as water fleas, they are a great food source for young and adult freshwater fish. A female will start to reproduce at 4 days old with a brood of 4 to 22 eggs. They get through the water by a hopping movement which is jerky in style.

Water Shrew

Neomys fodiens

Can live up to 14 months of age, their fur is a mixture of black and grey and can grow to about 62-95mm in length. They range throughout Europe except for Ireland, prefer fast flowing water that is clear but can also be found by ponds. The shrew are not endangered but are under threat in Britain due to loss of habitat.

Alder

Alnus Glutinosa

A fast growing hardy tree that thrives in wet conditions, but does not do well in dry conditions; it can cope with a wide range of soils and will grow well on damp hillsides and boggy water logged areas.

Bulrush
Typha

A tall marsh plant found in Eurasia (Europe and Asia), it grows in damp places and loves wet boggy soil. You can find them by lakes and ponds and their flowers, called catkins, release downy seeds which float away on a breeze

Blanket weed
Cladophora

This type of algae is sometimes known as string algae, mermaid hair or pond scum and causes the most concern in fresh water systems around the world. There are over 150 different species of *cladophora*. Algae can grow very fast when the conditions in a pond are just right; In very high levels of light, with high levels of nutrients, blanket weed and can grow at over 2 metres a day.

'Newton say's always be aware of water safety and be careful around ponds and rivers'.

New book coming soon:

Newton's Wildlife Adventures: A Load of Rubbish

Simon Knott

Children's book illustrator, model maker and teacher
I have studied illustration and hold a degree in model making from the well-respected UCA, Rochester as well as a PGCE in higher education from Greenwich University. Since this I have explored a wide range of different art mediums and have now developed a cartoon style utilising Photoshop on the computer. I love to put magic into children's books, covering science and nature with an environmental message.

www.simonrknott.com
siknotty@yahoo.co.uk

Stephanie Correll

Children's book writer
I have studied a HND in graphic and digital design and completed a short course in visual merchandising at The London College of Communication, having also worked with the prince's trust on a number of courses.
I am currently doing a STALIS course which hopefully will give me a greater chance to work with young children and have time with my young son, who is an inspiration for my writing. I enjoy the wildlife aspects, respect nature and enjoy the beauty it holds.

Stephanie.aspirations@googlemail.com